Rocio Martinez

MATTHEW

and the color of the sky

McGraw Hill **Wright Group**

for Antonio Ventura
for Verónica Uribe

translated by James A. Surges

Matías y el color del cielo by Rocío Martínez. First published in
Spanish by Ediciones Ekaré. Copyright © 2000 by Ediciones
Ekaré, Caracas, Venezuela.

www.WrightGroup.com

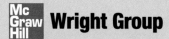 **Wright Group**

Printed in Mexico.

Send all inquiries to:
Wright Group/McGraw-Hill
P.O. Box 812960
Chicago, IL 60681

ISBN 978-0-07-658167-2
MHID 0-07-658167-5

4 5 6 7 8 9 DRN 16 15 14 13 12 11

Rocío Martínez

MATTHEW

and the color of the sky

Matthew is miffed.

The colors he wants to paint just won't come out right.

"What's the matter?" Penny asks.

"I want to paint the color of the sky, but it's always changing," complains Matthew.

"Can I help?" Penny asks.
"Sure, but it's hard," answers Matthew.

"I want to paint the color of the sky at dawn," says Matthew.

"Isn't it like the color of Juan's skin?" asks Penny.

"Yes! That's the color!" says Matthew.

"Now I want to paint the color of the sky when the sun is at its highest," says Matthew.

"Look at Trixie's chicks. Isn't that like the color of their feathers?" asks Penny.

"Yes, it is!" answers Matthew.

"I want to paint the color of a cloudy sky, too...

the color it has when it's raining," says Matthew.

"Isn't that like the color of Tina's hair?" Penny asks again.

"Yes, that's it!" says Matthew.

"Now, will you be able to paint the color of the sky when the sun has gone down?" asks Penny.
Matthew thinks about it.

"Yes! Of course!" Matthew exclaims. "That's the color of my own hair."

"Exactly," answers Penny.

"Gosh," thinks Matthew,

"the sky has a thousand colors."